Animals

Written by Jinny Johnson
Illustrated by Mike Atkinson

This is a Parragon Publishing Book
This edition published in 2001

Parragon Publishing
Queen Street House
4 Queen Street
Bath BA1 1HE, UK

Copyright © Parragon 1998

ISBN: 0 75254 834 4

Printed in Italy

Produced by Miles Kelly Publishing Ltd
Unit 11
Bardfield Centre
Great Bardfield
Essex
CM7 4SL

Contents

Dormouse

The dormouse normally weighs up to 1 oz (25 g), but it puts on extra fat before it hibernates.

Do dormice really sleep a lot?

Dormice do sleep through the winter. This hibernation may start in October and last until April, longer in cold climates. The dormouse sleeps in in a cozy nest on the ground or in a burrow.

Where do porcupines live?

There are two groups of porcupines. New World porcupines live in North and South America and live in trees. Old World porcupines live in Africa and parts of Asia. They are ground-dwelling animals. All porcupines are covered in long sharp spines, which look fearsome and help protect them from their enemies.

Why do beavers build dams?

BEAVERS BUILD THEIR HOMES—OR LODGES—IN STREAMS OR RIVERS. But first they need to build a dam to make an area of still water, or the current would wash the lodge away. With their huge front teeth, the beavers cut down trees to build the dam. They plaster the sides with mud and fill gaps with stones and sticks. The lodge is built of sticks behind the dam and has an underwater entrance. The beavers sleep, store food, and care for their young in the lodge. They have to keep repairing both the dam and the lodge with more sticks and mud. Beavers live in North America and in parts of Europe and Asia.

Porcupine

If attacked, the porcupine runs backward toward its enemy, driving in its sharp spines.

Which is the smallest rodent?

One of the smallest rodents is the pygmy mouse of North America. This is only about 4 in (10 cm) long, including its tail, and weighs 1/4 oz (7 g). The harvest mouse of Europe and Asia is only slightly bigger.

What do beavers eat?

Beavers eat plant food. In spring and summer they feed on fresh green leaves and grasses. In autumn they gather woody stems to eat. Some of these are stored under water near the lodge to keep fresh for the winter months.

How many kinds of rodent are there?

There are more than 1,600 different species of rodent, including squirrels, hamsters, and beavers as well as rats and mice. Rodents live all over the world in every kind of habitat from the icy Arctic to scorching deserts and humid rain forests.

Why do rodents get long in the tooth?

The two sharp teeth at the front of the rodent's jaw—called incisors—are the ones it uses for gnawing. A rodent's incisors get worn down as it gnaws tough food, but they keep on growing throughout its life.

Which is the biggest rodent?

The largest rodent in the world is the capybara, which lives in South America. It measures up to 53 in (1.3 metres) long and weighs up to 140 lb (64 kg). Capybaras live by water and feed on grasses.

How big is a beaver?

A fully grown beaver measures up to 67 in (1.7 metres) long, including its long flat tail. It weighs as much as 60 lb (27 kg) and is the second heaviest rodent in the world.

A beaver lodge

The beaver swims with the help of its webbed back feet and its large flattened tail.

Can flying squirrels really fly?

No, but they can glide some distance from tree to tree. When the flying squirrel leaps into the air, it stretches out the skin flaps at the sides of its body. These act like a parachute, enabling it to glide gently down from one branch to another.

Is a guinea pig a rodent?

A guinea pig is a rodent. Wild guinea pigs, also known as cavies, live in South America, where they feed on leaves and grasses. Most cavies are about 9 in (22 cm) long, but one type, the long-legged, harelike mara, is up to 30 in (75 cm) long.

When is a dog really a rat?

A PRAIRIE DOG IS ACTUALLY NOT A DOG AT ALL. IN FACT IT'S A TYPE OF RODENT, and lives in North America. Each prairie dog family, called a coterie, makes a burrow of connecting chambers and tunnels. A coterie contains one adult male and up to four females and their young. Groups of coteries live near each other in huge areas of burrows called towns. Prairie dogs feed mostly on grasses and other plants. While the family is feeding, one prairie dog keeps watch. It barks loudly to warn the others of any danger.

The living chamber in the beaver's lodge is above the water level.

How many kinds of bear are there?

THERE ARE EIGHT SPECIES OF BEAR. THEY RANGE IN SIZE FROM THE SUN BEAR, which weighs only about 60 lb (27 kg), to huge polar bears and brown bears. The brown bear is the most widespread bear. It lives in northern North America and parts of Europe and Asia. In North America the brown bear is sometimes called the grizzly. Brown bears have a varied diet. They eat grasses, roots, and berries, but they also catch insects, fish, and other larger animals, as well as scavenging the carcasses of dead creatures such as deer and seals.

The panda's front paws have a special extra digit to help it grip bamboo stems.

Which is the biggest bear?
The polar bear, which lives in the Arctic. Fully grown males are up to 8.5 ft (2.6 meters) long. Polar bears have thick white fur to keep them warm in their icy home. They hunt seals and occasionally also young walrus and birds.

Is the giant panda a bear?
For many years experts argued about whether this animal should be grouped with bears or raccoons or classed in a separate family of its own. Genetic evidence now suggests that the panda is a member of the bear family.

What do giant pandas eat?
The main food of the giant panda is bamboo. An adult panda eats up to 33 lb (15 kg) of bamboo leaves and stems a day. Pandas also eat a small amount of other plants and even some little animals.

How many kinds of wild dog are there?
There are about 35 species in the dog family, including foxes, wolves, coyotes, and hunting dogs. Wild dogs live all over the world, except in New Zealand, New Guinea, and a few other islands. All are good runners and hunt other animals to eat.

A red fox is up to 25 in (63 cm) long, with a bushy tail of up to 16 in (40 cm). Foxes live and hunt in an area called a territory, which they mark with their scent.

Where do giant pandas live?
Giant pandas live in bamboo forests in the mountains of central China. Most of these forests have now been made into special reserves to try and protect the rare pandas. Some pandas also live in captivity in zoos in China and other countries.

Red fox

What do foxes eat?
Foxes, such as the red fox, are hunting animals. They kill and eat small creatures, including rats, mice, and rabbits. But foxes are very adaptable—they will eat more or less anything that comes their way, such as birds and birds' eggs, insects, and even fruit and berries. And more and more foxes in cities are feasting on our discarded food from garbage cans and compost heaps.

How big is a wolf pack?

In areas where there are plenty of large animals to catch, a pack may contain up to 20 wolves. Hunting in a pack means that the wolves can kill prey much larger than themselves, such as moose. A wolf pack has a home range, or territory, which it defends against other wolves.

How do wolf cubs learn how to hunt?

Wolf cubs learn how to hunt by watching their parents and other pack members and by playing. As the cubs run around and pounce on one another, they are also learning how to attack and ambush prey.

Can polar bears swim?

Polar bears can swim well and spend long periods in the freezing Arctic water. They are well equipped to survive the cold. A polar bear has a dense layer of underfur as well as a heavy, glossy outer coat. Under the skin is a thick layer of fat to give further protection.

Are there bears in the jungle?

Yes, there are two kinds of bear that live in jungle, or rain forest. Some spectacled bears live in South American rain forest, and the sun bear lives in rain forest in parts of Southeast Asia.

How big is a baby bear?

Although adult bears are so big, they have tiny babies. A huge polar bear, weighing more than several people, gives birth to cubs of only about 28 oz (800 g), far smaller than most human babies. Baby pandas are tinier still. The mother weighs up to 220 lb (100 kg) but her newborn cubs are only 3–5 oz (85–140 g).

What is a dingo?

Dingoes are wild dogs that live in Australia. They are descended from dogs domesticated more than 3,500 years ago by the earliest aboriginal inhabitants. They live in family groups and hunt sheep and rabbits. A fence 3,307 miles (5,322 km) long has been built across southeastern Australia to try to keep dingoes out of important sheep-grazing lands.

Brown bear

A male brown bear stands up to 84 in (213 cm) tall and weighs up to 838 lb (380 kg). Bears like plant food and will reach up into trees to pick juicy fruit or berries.

Do bears sleep through the winter?

BROWN BEARS AND AMERICAN AND ASIAN BLACK BEARS THAT LIVE IN THE far north do sleep for much of the winter. Food supplies are poor and the bears hide themselves away in warm dens and live off their own fat reserves. Before their long sleep and fast, the bears eat as much food as they can to build up their body fat. They may not eat or drink again for as long as six months. A bear's body temperature drops only slightly during the winter sleep and it wakes easily if disturbed. Female bears may give birth to a litter of cubs during this time.

Meerkats on guard

Meerkats thrive in the hostile Kalahari desert by working as a team. A group of adults watch out for predators while others are out hunting.

What is a meerkat?

A meerkat is a type of mongoose, which lives in Africa. Meerkats form large groups of up to 30 or more animals, which share the guarding of young and finding of food. Sentry meerkats often stand up on their hind legs to watch out for danger.

Which cat runs the fastest?

The cheetah is the fastest running cat and one of the speediest of all animals over short distances. It has been timed running at 60 mph (105 kph) over 110 yds (100 meters). Olympic sprinters can reach only about 30 mph (48 kph).

What is a panther?

A panther is simply a leopard with a black coat instead of spots. It is not a separate species of cat. Leopards live in Africa and Asia.

What does a mongoose eat?

The mongoose is a fast-moving little hunter. It will kill small creatures such as rats, mice, and frogs and will also take anything else it can find, including insects and birds' eggs. A mongoose will even tackle a large snake.

How many kinds of cat are there?

There are about 35 species of wild cat, ranging from the tiger to the African wild cat, which is the main ancestor of domestic cats. Cats live in most parts of the world in every sort of habitat from tropical rainforest and desert to the icy lands of Siberia. There are no wild cats in Antarctica, Australia, or New Zealand.

The pattern of stripes on a tiger's skin is unique. No two tigers have quite the same pattern.

Tiger

Which big cat is the biggest?

TIGERS ARE THE BIGGEST OF THE BIG CATS. THEY MEASURE UP TO 10 FT (3 METERS) long, including the tail, and weigh 550 lb (250 kg) or more. Tigers are becoming very rare. They live in parts of Asia, from snowy Siberia in the north to the tropical rain forests of Sumatra. There is only one species of tiger, but those in the north tend to be larger and have thicker, lighter colored fur than their relations farther south. Tigers live alone, coming together only for mating. The female rears her cubs without the help of her mate. At first the cubs stay close to the den, but when they are about six months old they begin to go with their mother on hunts and learn how to find food for themselves.

What do lions do all day?

Like domestic cats, lions are actually asleep for a surprisingly large part of the day. As many as 22 hours a day are spent resting and grooming. The rest of the time is taken up with looking for prey, hunting, and feeding. Lionesses do most of the hunting, but they share the catch with the rest of the pride.

Where do jaguars live?

Jaguars live in the forests of Central and South America. They are the largest South American cats and measure up to 6 ft (1.8 meters) long with a tail of up to 36 in (90 cm). Despite its size, the jaguar is a good climber and often clambers up a tree to watch for prey. It hunts other forest animals such as peccaries and capybaras as well as birds, turtles, and fish.

Why are lions unlike other cats?

MOST CATS LIVE ALONE. LIONS LIVE AND HUNT IN A GROUP CALLED A PRIDE. Tigers, cheetahs, and other big cats live alone, unless rearing young. A lion pride includes several adult males and a number of females, young lions, and cubs. Living in a group means that there are always some adults to look after the cubs while others are off hunting. And working together, lions can bring down animals much larger than themselves, such as wildebeest and zebra.

What is a snow leopard?

The snow leopard is a big cat that lives in the Himalaya Mountains. It has a beautiful pale coat with dark markings, which has made it the target of fur poachers. Killing snow leopards for their fur is now illegal, but poaching still goes on.

How different are our pet cats from wild cats?

Pet cats and wild cats have exactly the same body structure and skeleton. Both rely heavily on smell for information about the world and they mark their territories by spraying urine or by rubbing the body against trees or other objects. All cats are meat eaters and cannot live on a diet of plant foods.

Is a civet a kind of cat?

No, civets belong to a separate family, which also includes mongooses, meerkats, and genets. Most civets live in tropical forests in Southeast Asia or Africa. They have a long, slender body, short legs and a long tail. The African civet is about 37 in (95 cm) long with a tail of about 20 in (50 cm). It hunts small mammals, birds, reptiles, and insects.

Why do tigers have stripes?

A tiger's stripes help it hide among grasses and leaves so it can surprise its prey. Tigers cannot run fast for long distances so they depend on being able to get close to their prey before making the final pounce. The stripes help to break up their outline and make them hard for prey to see.

How long are an elephant's tusks?

An elephant's tusks grow throughout its life, so the oldest elephants have the longest tusks. An old male elephant may have tusks that measure up to 11 ft (3.5 meters) and weigh 264 lb (120 kg).

An elephant's tusks are actually very long upper teeth.

African elephant

How much do elephants eat?

A fully grown elephant eats 220 to 440 lb (100 to 200 kg) of plant food a day, including grass, twigs, branches, leaves, flowers, and fruits.

What do elephants do with their trunks?

THE ELEPHANT'S TRUNK IS VERY USEFUL. WITHOUT IT, AN ELEPHANT could not reach the ground to feed because its neck is so short. The trunk is also used for taking food from high in the trees and for breaking off branches. The elephant can smell with its trunk, pick up tiny objects, and gently caress its young. It drinks by sucking up water into its trunk and squirting it into its mouth. It also sprays water or dust over itself to clean its skin.

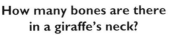

Giraffe

The elephant flaps its huge ears to help keep itself cool.

The giraffe's tongue can stretch out up to 18 in (46 cm) to help it gather leaves from tall trees.

How tall is a giraffe?
A male giraffe stands up to 18 ft (5.5 meters) tall to the tips of its horns. It has an extraordinarily long neck, and front legs that are longer than its back legs so the body slopes down toward the tail. The long neck allows it to feed on leaves high in trees that other animals cannot reach.

How many bones are there in a giraffe's neck?
A giraffe has seven bones in its neck, just like other mammals, including humans. But the giraffe's neck bones are much longer than those of other animals, and have more flexible joints between them.

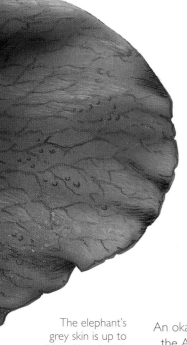

The elephant's grey skin is up to 1½ in (4 cm) thick and has a fine covering of hairs.

What is an okapi?
An okapi is a relative of the giraffe that lives in the African rain forest. It was discovered as recently as 1901 by a British explorer. It has small horns on its head and a long tongue like a giraffe's—but it does not have a long neck.

Are rhinoceroses fierce animals?
Despite their ferocious appearance and huge horns, rhinos are peaceful, plant-eating animals. But if threatened, a rhino will charge its enemy, galloping at high speed with its huge head held down ready to attack. Mothers defending their young can be particularly dangerous.

Can hippos swim?
The hippo spends most of its day in or near water and comes out on to land at night to feed on plants. It does not really swim, but it walks or runs along underwater or on the bottom of the river at surprising speeds.

How can you tell an African elephant from an Asian elephant?

THE AFRICAN ELEPHANT IS BIGGER AND HAS LARGER EARS AND LONGER TUSKS. The head and body of the African elephant measures up to 24.5 ft (7.5 meters) long. The Asian elephant measures up to 21 ft (6.5 meters) and has a more humped back. There is another difference at the end of the long trunk. The African elephant's trunk has two flexible fingerlike lips, while the Asian animal's trunk has only one.

How big is a baby elephant?
A newborn baby elephant weighs up to 264 lb (120 kg) and stands up to 40 in (1 meter) high. It feeds on its mother's milk for at least two years, by which time it may weigh more than 1,322 lb (600 kg), and it may continue suckling for up to six years.

Do all marsupials live in Australia?

Most of the 260 or so species of marsupial live in Australia and New Guinea, but there are about 80 species of marsupial opossum in South America. One of these also lives in North America.

Which is the smallest marsupial?

The smallest marsupials are the mouselike ningauis, which live in Australia. These little creatures are only about 2 in (5 cm) long and weigh only a few grams. They feed on insects.

Do all marsupials have a pouch?

Most female marsupials have a pouch, but not all. Some very small marsupials such as the shrew opossums of South America do not have a pouch. Others, such as the American opossums, simply have flaps of skin around the nipples and not a full pouch. The tiny young cling on to the nipples.

Do any marsupials swim?

The water opossum, which lives in South America, is an excellent swimmer and has webbed back feet. Strong muscles keep its pouch closed when the opossum is in water.

Why does a kangaroo have a pouch?

AT BIRTH, KANGAROOS ARE VERY TINY AND EXTREMELY POORLY DEVELOPED. In fact, a kangaroo is only about $^3/_4$ in (2 cm) long when it is born. The female kangaroo has a pouch so that its young can complete their development in safety. The tiny newborn crawls up to the pouch by itself and starts to suckle on one of the nipples inside the pouch. A young kangaroo, or joey, stays in the pouch until it weighs about 20 lb (9 kg). Pouched animals like kangaroos are called marsupials.

How many kinds of kangaroo and wallaby are there?

There are about 60 different species of kangaroo and wallaby. All live in Australia or New Guinea. The red kangaroo, which weighs about 198 lb (90 kg), is the largest, and the tiny musky rat kangaroo, weighing only 1.2 lb (0.5 kg), is the smallest.

What do kangaroos eat?

Kangaroos eat grass and the leaves of low-growing plants, just like deer and antelopes do in the northern hemisphere.

Red kangaroo

Only the male red kangaroo has a reddish coat. Females are bluish-gray.

What is a Tasmanian devil?

The Tasmanian devil is the largest of the carnivores, or flesh-eating marsupials. It is about 36 in (90 cm) long, including its tail, and has sharp teeth and strong jaws. The devil feeds mostly on carrion—the flesh of animals that are already dead—but it does also kill prey such as sheep and birds.

How much does a koala eat every day?

A koala eats about 1 lb (500 g) of eucalyptus leaves every day, which it chews down to a fine pulp with its broad teeth. The leaves do not provide much energy, but koalas are slow-moving animals and sleep up to 18 hours a day.

Is a platypus a marsupial?

No, the platypus is not a marsupial, but it is an unusual animal and it does live in Australia. Unlike most mammals, which give birth to live young, the platypus lays eggs. The mother leaves her two or three eggs to incubate in a burrow for up to two weeks. When they hatch, the young feed on the milk that flows from openings in the mother's body.

What are bandicoots?

Bandicoots are a group of small marsupials that live in Australia and New Guinea. Most have short legs, a rounded body and a long pointed nose. They have strong claws, which they use to dig worms and other small creatures from the ground.

Koala bear

The koala has strong claws to help it hold on to branches as it climbs in search of food.

Is a koala really a kind of bear?

NO, IT'S A MARSUPIAL LIKE A KANGAROO AND NOT RELATED TO BEARS AT ALL. Koalas live in Australia in eucalyptus forests. They feed almost entirely on eucalyptus leaves, preferring those of only a few species. A baby koala spends its first six or seven months in the pouch and then rides on its mother's back until it is able to fend for itself. A baby weighs less than half a gram at birth, but when fully grown the average koala measures about 30 in (78 cm) long and weighs up to 24 lb (11 kg). Females are much smaller than males.

How fast do kangaroos move?

A kangaroo bounds along on its strong back legs at up to 40 mph (65 kph). It can cover 39 ft (12 meters) in one bound.

What is a wombat?

A wombat is a small bearlike marsupial with a heavy body and short strong legs. It digs burrows to shelter in and feeds mostly on grass. Its pouch opens to the rear so that it does not fill up with earth when the wombat is burrowing.

What do gorillas eat?

Gorillas eat plant food, such as leaves, buds, stems, and fruit. Because their diet is juicy, gorillas rarely need to drink.

Which is the smallest monkey?

The smallest monkey is the pygmy marmoset, which lives in South American rain forest. It is about 15 in (40 cm) long, but half of this is tail, and it weighs only about 5 oz (150 g).

Gorillas usually move on all fours, leaning on the knuckles of their front limbs.

What is an ape?

Apes are the most advanced animals in the primate group, which also includes animals such as lemurs, bush babies, and monkeys. There, are three families of apes. One includes all the different kinds of gibbons. The second contains the gorilla, chimpanzee, and orangutan and the third has one species only—humans.

Where do orangutans live?

Orangutans live in Southeast Asia in the rain forests of Sumatra and Borneo. This ape has long reddish fur and spends most of its life in the trees. Fruit is its main food but the orangutan also eats leaves, insects, and even eggs and small animals. The orangutan is active during the day. At night it sleeps on the ground or in a nest of branches in the trees.

Which is the biggest ape?

THE GORILLA—A FULLY GROWN MALE STANDS UP TO 5.5 FT (1.7 METERS) TALL and weighs as much as 400 lb (180 kg). Gorillas live in rain forest in West and Central Africa. A family group contains an adult male, several females and a number of young of different ages. The male, known as a silverback because of the white hair on his back, leads the group.

Gorilla family

Do chimpanzees hunt prey?

Yes they do. Although fruit is the main food of chimpanzees, they also eat insects and hunt young animals such as monkeys. Male chimpanzees usually do the hunting. They work together in a group, some cutting a couple of animals out of the herd and driving them toward other chimps, who will make the kill. The rest of the troop then joins in to share the meat.

Chimpanzee

An adult chimpanzee is up to 33 in (85 cm) long and does not have a tail.

Why does the monkey have a long tail?

To help it balance and control its movements as it leaps from branch to branch in the rain forest. The tails of South American monkeys are even more useful than those of their African and Asian relatives, because they are prehensile. A prehensile tail has special muscles that the monkey can use to twine round branches and help it climb—it's almost like having a fifth leg. The naked skin on the underside of the tail is ridged to improve grip.

Chimpanzees climb well and find much of their food in trees.

Do chimpanzees use tools?

Yes. The chimpanzee can get food by poking a stick into an ants' nest. It pulls out the stick and licks off the ants. It also uses stones to crack nuts, and it makes sponges from chewed leaves to mop up water or wipe its body.

Which monkey makes the loudest noise?

Howler monkeys not only shout louder than other monkeys—they are among the noisiest of all animals. Troops of monkeys call to each other and their voices carry for more than 0.6 miles (1 km).

Do any monkeys live in cold places?

Most monkeys are found in warm areas near the equator, but some macaque monkeys live in cooler places. The rhesus macaque lives in the Himalayas as well as in parts of China and India, and the Japanese macaque survives freezing winters with the help of its thick coat.

How many kinds of monkey are there?

About 133 species in three main groups. One group lives in Africa and Asia. The other two groups live in Central and South America.

Do chimpanzees live in family groups?

Yes, in very large families that may include between 25 and 100 animals, led by a dominant male. Each group has its own home range.

Where do chimpanzees live?

Chimpanzees live in forest and grasslands in West and Central Africa. There is another less familiar chimpanzee species called the pygmy chimpanzee, or bonobo, which lives in rain forests in Zaire/Congo in Africa. It is slimmer and lighter than the common chimpanzee and spends more of its time in trees.

Californian sea lion

How can you tell a seal from a sea lion?

WITH PRACTICE! SEALS AND SEA LIONS BOTH HAVE STREAMLINED BODIES adapted to marine living, and flippers instead of limbs. But there are several differences between them. Sea lions have small ear flaps, but seals have only ear openings, no flaps. Sea lions can bring their back flippers under the body to help them move on land. Seals cannot do this—they simply drag themselves along. Sea lions swim by moving their front flippers. Seals swim by moving the back flippers and the rear of the body.

The sea lion tucks its back flippers under itself when on land.

How do seals keep warm in cold sea?

A layer of fatty blubber under the skin helps to keep seals and sea lions warm. The blubber may be up to 4 in (10 cm) thick. These animals also have a covering of fur.

How fast do seals and sea lions swim?

A Californian sea lion has been timed swimming at 25 mph (40 kph). On land the crabeater seal can move at up to 11 mph (19 kph) as it toboggans over ice.

How deep do seals dive?

The Weddell seal, which lives in Antarctic waters, is one of the deepest-diving seals. It can go down to depths of more than 1,640 ft (500 meters) in search of food. When the seal dives, blood flow is cut off to all but essential organs such as the heart.

How big are sea lions?

The biggest, the steller sea lion, is about 90 in (230 cm) long and weighs as much as 2,200 lb (1,000 kg). Females are much smaller and weigh only about 595 lb (270 kg). The smallest is probably the Galapagos fur seal, which weighs only about 140 lb (64 kg).

Are baby seals and sea lions born in water?

No, they are born on land. Seals and sea lions spend most of their lives in water but they do come out on to land to give birth. They remain on land for a number of weeks, feeding their young on their rich milk.

Harp seal

Which is the smallest seal?

The ringed seal is one of the smallest seals. The male grows to about 4.5 ft (1.4 meters) long and weighs up to 198 lb (90 kg), although some are only 110 lb (50 kg). Females are slightly smaller than males. Ringed seals live in Arctic waters and eat fish and shellfish.

How big is a walrus?

The largest male walruses are more than 10 ft (3 meters) long and weigh 2,645 lb (1,200 kg). Females are smaller, averaging 9 ft (2.7 meters) long and weighing about 1,760 lb (800 kg) The walrus's skin is up to 1½ in (4 cm) thick and covered with coarse hairs. The thick skin helps protect the walrus from the tusks of others.

Do seals live in fresh water?

Yes, there is a species of freshwater seal in Lake Baikal in Russia. Baikal is the deepest freshwater lake in the world and holds more water than any other. Thousands of seals live there, feeding on freshwater fish and resting on the remote islands in the middle of the lake.

How long are a walrus's tusks?

The tusks of an adult male walrus can be up to 22 in (55 cm) long. Some people think that a walrus uses its tusks to dig shellfish from the seabed, but other experts believe that the tusks are just for display and attracting mates.

Are any seals very rare?

Yes, monk seals, which live in the Caribbean, Mediterranean, and Hawaiian seas, are extremely rare. The Caribbean seal is probably already extinct. These are the only seals that live in warm seas, closer to human activity than other seals, so they have suffered greater habitat disturbance.

Which is the biggest seal?

The male elephant seal is the biggest of all the seals. It is 5 meters (16 ft) long and weighs 2,400 kg (5,300 lb), nearly as much as an elephant.

How many kinds of seal and sea lion are there?

There are about 14 species of sea lion, 18 species of seal, and one species of walrus. Most sea lions live along North Pacific coasts and on the southern coasts of Africa, Australia and South America. Most seals live in waters to the far north and south of the world, and the walrus lives in Arctic seas.

What do seals and sea lions eat?

FISH IS THEIR MAIN DIET, BUT SOME ALSO EAT SHELLFISH AND CATCH LARGER PREY. Some seals have a more varied diet. The crabeater seal feeds mostly on krill, small shrimplike crustaceans. The bearded seal eats seabed creatures such as clams, and the leopard seal preys on the young of other seals as well as birds and fish.

Do seals and sea lions breathe air?

Seals and sea lions are mammals so they have to come to the surface regularly to breathe air. But they can stay underwater much longer than we can. Dives lasting 20 minutes or more are common and the Weddell seal has been timed making a dive of over 70 minutes.

Fur seals have extra-thick fur and look like true seals. But their small ear flaps show they are really types of sea lion.

Dolphins

How big is a baby blue whale?
A baby blue whale is about 23 ft (7 meters) long at birth and is the biggest baby in the animal kingdom. It weighs about 8 tons—that is more than a fully grown elephant.

Which is the biggest whale?

THE BLUE WHALE IS THE LARGEST WHALE, AND ALSO THE LARGEST MAMMAL THAT has ever lived. It measures more than 100 ft (30 meters) long. It weighs at least 100 tons and the biggest blue whales may weigh more than twice this amount. Although it is so huge, the blue whale is not a fierce hunter. It eats tiny shrimplike creatures called krill. It may gobble up as many as four million of these in a day.

Dolphins leap out of the water as they swim and dive back in head first.

What is a porpoise?
A porpoise is a small whale with a rounded head, not a beaked snout like a dolphin. There are about six species of porpoise, which live in coastal waters in the Atlantic and Pacific. They feed on fish and squid.

Which whale dives deepest?
The sperm whale dives to at least 3,300 ft (1,000 meters) below the surface of the sea and may go down to even greater depths when chasing giant squid to eat.

Do whales ever come to land?
No, whales spend their whole lives in the sea. But they do breathe air and have to come to the surface regularly to take breaths.

Blue whales once lived in all oceans. Now most are found in Antarctic waters.

Blue whale

Is a dolphin a kind of whale?

A DOLPHIN IS A SMALL WHALE. MOST OF THE 37 OR SO SPECIES OF DOLPHIN live in the sea, but there are five that live in rivers. The biggest dolphin is usually known as the killer whale, or orca, and grows up to 31 ft (9.4 meters) long. Dolphins have a streamlined shape and a beaked snout containing lots of sharp teeth. They are fast swimmers and they catch sea creatures such as fish and squid to eat. A form of ultrasound helps dolphins find their prey. A dolphin gives off a series of high-frequency clicking sounds that bounce off anything in their path. The echoes tell the dolphin about the size and direction of the prey.

Do whales give birth in the water?
Yes, they do. The baby whale comes out of the mother's body tail first so that it does not drown during birth. As soon as the head emerges, the mother and the other females attending the birth help the baby whale swim to the surface to take its first breath.

What is a narwhal?
A narwhal is a whale with a single long tusk at the front of its head. The tusk is actually a tooth, which grows out from the upper jaw. It can be as much as 9 ft (2.7 meters) long. Only male narwhals have tusks and they may use them in battles with other males.

Do humpback whales really sing?
Yes, they do. They make a series of sounds, including high whistles and low rumbles, that may continue for hours. No one knows exactly why the humpback whale sings, but it may be to court a mate or to keep in touch with others in the group.

Why do some whales migrate?
Whales such as humpbacks migrate—travel from place to place—to find the best conditions for feeding and breeding. They spend much of the year feeding in the waters of the Arctic and Antarctic, where there is lots of krill to eat. When it is time to give birth, the humpbacks travel to warmer waters near the equator.

How fast do whales swim?
Blue whales normally swim at about 5 mph (8 kph) but can move at speeds of up to 18 mph (30 kph) when disturbed. Some small whales, such as pilot whales and dolphins, may swim at more than 30 mph (50 kph).

How does a blue whale feed?
A blue whale filters small shrimplike creatures called krill from the water. Hanging from the whale's upper jaw are lots of plates of a fringed bristly material called baleen. The whale opens its mouth and water, and krill, flows in. The whale forces the water through the baleen with its tongue. The water flows out at the sides of the mouth, leaving the krill behind on the baleen for the whale to swallow.

Puffer fish

How fast do fish swim?
The sailfish is one of the fastest swimming fish. It has been timed moving at speeds of more than 62 mph (100 kph). Marlins and tunas are also fast swimmers. All these fish have sleek streamlined bodies.

This fish puffs up its body when in danger.

Does a stingray sting?
A stingray gets its name from the sharp spine near the base of its tail. This carries poison and causes a nasty wound if the fish drives it into the flesh of its enemy. It can even kill a human.

Are flatfishes born flat?
No, they are not. Young flatfishes have normal bodies with an eye on each side. As they grow, the body flattens and one eye moves, so that both are on the upper surface. The fish lies on the seabed with its eyed side uppermost so it can see.

Are there any poisonous fish?

YES, THERE ARE—AND THE PUFFER FISH IS ONE OF THE MOST POISONOUS OF ALL. It has a powerful poison in some of its internal organs, such as the heart and liver, which can kill a human. Despite this, puffer fish is a delicacy in Japan, where chefs are specially trained to remove the poisonous parts and prepare the fish. A puffer fish also has another way of defending itself. It can puff its body up with water and air until it is at least twice its normal size. This makes it very hard for any predator to swallow. Some puffer fish are covered with spines that stick up when the body is inflated.

Which is the fiercest freshwater fish?
The piranha, which lives in rivers in tropical Central and South America, is the fiercest of all freshwater fish. Each fish is only about 12 in (30 cm) long, but a shoal of hundreds attacking together can kill and eat a much larger animal in seconds. The piranha's weapons are its extremely sharp triangular-shaped teeth, which it uses to chop flesh from its victim. But not all piranhas are dangerous killers. Some species feed only on plants.

How many kinds of shark are there?
There are about 370 different species of shark living all over the world. They range in size from tiny fish only 10 in (25 cm) long, to the giant whale shark, which can grow to 50 ft (15 meters).

Are electric eels really electric?
Yes, they are. The electric eel's body contains special muscles that can release electrical charges into the water. These are powerful enough to stun and kill its prey.

Why does a flying fish "fly"?
A flying fish usually lifts itself above the water to escape from danger. It has extra large fins, which act as its "wings". After building up speed in the water, the fish lifts its fins and glides above the surface for a short distance.

How big is a great white shark?

GREAT WHITE SHARKS ARE MOSTLY ABOUT 23 FT (7 METERS) LONG, but some can grow up to 40 ft (12 meters). They live in warm seas all over the world. Great white sharks are fierce hunters and attack large fish and other creatures such as sea lions and porpoises. Their main weapons are their large, jagged-edged teeth, which they use to kill prey and to tear it apart. Behind these teeth are rows of new ones, ready to replace teeth at the front that get damaged or broken.

Great white shark

The shark's teeth may be up to 3 in (7.5 cm) long.

Are all sharks killers?
No, two of the largest sharks, the whale shark and the basking shark, eat only tiny shrimplike creatures. They filter these from the water through special sievelike structures in the mouth.

A shark may swim at speeds of up to 25 mph (40 kph) for short periods.

Poison-arrow frog

The poison-arrow frog is one of the most poisonous of all animals.

Do all frogs lay their eggs in water?
No, some frogs have very unusual breeding habits. The male marsupial frog, for example, carries his mate's eggs on his back. A layer of skin grows over them to protect them. The male Darwin's frog keeps his mate's eggs in his mouth until they have developed into tiny frogs.

What do frogs eat?
Adult frogs catch insects and spiders and other small creatures such as crayfish and even other frogs to eat. Tadpoles usually feed on small water plants.

What is an amphibian?
An amphibian is a creature that lives in water and on land. Amphibians evolved from fish and were the first vertebrates (creatures with backbones) to live on land. There are about 3,000 species of amphibian, including frogs, toads, newts, and salamanders.

What is a tadpole?
A tadpole is the young, or larva, of an amphibian such as a frog or newt. The amphibian egg is usually laid in water and hatches out into a small, swimming creature with a long tail called a tadpole. The tadpole feeds on water plants and gradually develops into its adult form.

Why do frogs croak?
Male frogs make their croaking calls to attract females. The frog has a special sac of skin under its chin, which blows up and helps make the call louder.

Which is the smallest frog?
The smallest frog, and the smallest of all amphibians, is the Cuban frog, which measures only $^3/_8$ in long. The tiny gold frog, which lives in Brazilian rainforests, is only slightly bigger at about $^3/_4$ in (2 cm) long.

Are frogs and toads poisonous?

SOME ARE—THE CANE TOAD CAN SQUIRT POISON AT AN ENEMY FROM GLANDS near its eyes, and the fire-bellied toad has poison in its skin. But most deadly of all are the poison-arrow frogs that live in South American rain forests. Their skin contains one of the most powerful poisons known and a tiny drop can kill a person. Local people tip their hunting arrows with this deadly substance by simply rubbing the arrow over the skin of a frog. Poison-arrow frogs live in trees and are usually very brightly colored. Their bold markings warn predators that they are poisonous and should be left alone. But there is a frog-eating snake in the rain forest that seems to be able to eat the frogs without coming to any harm.

How can treefrogs climb trees?
Treefrogs are excellent climbers. On each of their long toes is a round sticky pad, which allows them to cling to the undersides of leaves and to run up the smoothest surfaces. Treefrogs spend most of their lives in trees, catching insects to eat, and only come down to the ground to lay their eggs in water.

How did the spadefoot toad get its name?
The spadefoot toad got its name from the hard spadelike projection on each back foot, which it uses for digging its burrow. The toad backs into the ground, pushing soil away with its "spades". It usually spends the day deep in its burrow and comes out at night to find food.

Can the flying frog really fly?

NO, BUT IT CAN GLIDE 40 FT (12 METERS) THROUGH THE AIR BETWEEN TREES. When the frog jumps into the air it stretches out its legs and toes so that its webbed feet act like little parachutes. Small flaps of skin on the legs also help the frog to glide. The flying frog lives in rain forests in Southeast Asia and spends most of its life in trees. Being able to "fly" in this way means that it does not have to go down to the ground and climb back up again to move from tree to tree.

How many types of frog and toad are there?

There are about 2,500 species of frog and toad. They live on all continents except Antarctica. Most live in areas with plenty of rainfall, but some manage to live in drier lands by sheltering in burrows.

Flaps of skin help the frog glide through the air.

Flying frog

How big is a giant toad?

The giant toad, which lives in parts of the southern United States, is up to 9½ in (24 cm) long. It eats beetles. It has been introduced into many parts of the world by farmers, in an effort to control the beetles that eat crops such as sugarcane.

What is a salamander?

A salamander looks like a lizard with its long body and tail, but it is an amphibian like frogs and toads. There are about 350 different kinds. The biggest is the giant salamander, which can grow to 5 ft (1.5 meters) long.

How can you tell a crocodile from an alligator?

You can recognize a crocodile because its teeth stick out when its mouth is shut!

In many ways, crocodiles and alligators are very similar. They both have long bodies covered with thick scales. And they both have long jaws with lots of sharp teeth. But when they shut their mouths, there is one difference between them that is easily spotted. In alligators, the fourth pair of teeth on the lower jaw disappears into pits in the upper jaws, but in crocodiles, these teeth slide outside the mouth into notches in the upper jaw, and can be seen when the mouth is closed.

Which is the biggest crocodile?

The Nile crocodile grows up to 19.5 ft (6 meters) long, but the Indopacific crocodile is even larger. This crocodile, which lives in parts of Southeast Asia, grows to 23 ft (7 meters) or more.

Do crocodiles lay eggs?

Crocodiles do lay eggs and they look after them very carefully. The female crocodile digs a pit into which she lays 30 or more eggs. She covers them over with earth or sand. While the eggs incubate for about three months, the female crocodile stays nearby guarding the nest. When the young hatch, the mother hears their cries and lifts them out of the pit with her mouth.

What do crocodiles eat?

Baby crocodiles start by catching insects and spiders to eat. As they grow, fish and birds form a larger part of their diet. Fully grown crocodiles prey on anything that comes their way, even large animals such as giraffes. The crocodile lies in the water near where animals come to drink, then suddenly lurches forward to seize the prey.

How big is a giant tortoise?
Giant tortoises grow up to 4.5 ft (1.4 meters) long and weigh as much as 550 lb (250 kg). They live on the Galapagos Islands in the Pacific and on the island of Aldabra in the Indian Ocean. Seychelles giant tortoises were thought to be extinct in the wild—to have died out completely—but some living animals have recently been discovered. Efforts are being made to breed more tortoises in captivity and release them into the wild.

Which is the biggest turtle?
The leatherback is the largest of all the turtles. It grows up to 64 in (1.6 meters) long and weighs up to 794 lb (360 kg). Leatherbacks also dive deeper than other turtles. They plunge down to more than 3,300 ft (1,000 meters).

What do sea turtles eat?
Most sea turtles eat a range of underwater creatures, such as clams, shrimps and snails, but some concentrate on certain foods. The hawksbill is one of the few creatures that feeds mostly on sponges. The leatherback's main food is jellyfish, while the green turtle eats sea grass.

The green turtle's broad shell is up to 5 ft (1.5 meters) long. Turtles "fly" through the water with the help of their paddle-shaped flippers.

Green turtle

Do turtles ever come to land?

SEA TURTLES SPEND NEARLY ALL THEIR LIVES IN THE WATER, BUT FEMALES do come to land to lay their eggs. The female green turtle drags herself up on to a sandy beach and digs a deep pit. She lays 100 or more eggs and covers them with sand. She then returns to the sea. When the young hatch, they must dig their own way out of the pit and struggle down the beach to the sea. Sadly, many get gobbled up by seabirds and other hunters before they reach the water.

Nile crocodile

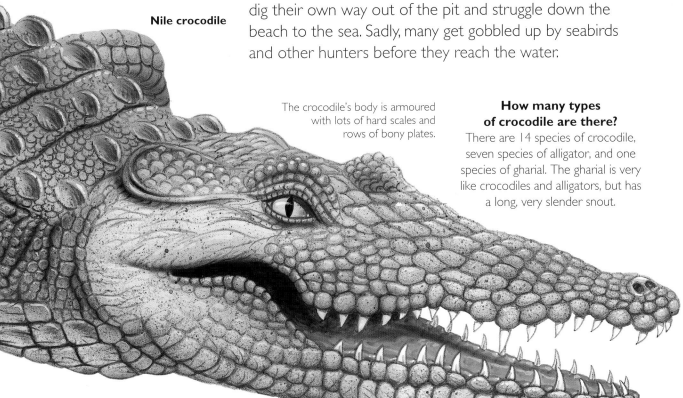

The crocodile's body is armoured with lots of hard scales and rows of bony plates.

How many types of crocodile are there?
There are 14 species of crocodile, seven species of alligator, and one species of gharial. The gharial is very like crocodiles and alligators, but has a long, very slender snout.

Which is the most dangerous snake?
The saw-scaled carpet viper is probably the world's most dangerous snake. It is extremely aggressive and its poison can kill humans. Saw-scaled carpet vipers live in Africa and Asia.

How fast do snakes move?
The fastest-moving snake on land is thought to be the black mamba, which lives in Africa. It can wriggle along at up to 12 mph (19 kph).

Reticulated python

The python can coil its strong body around its prey and crush it to death.

Are there any snakes in the sea?
Yes, there are about 47 different species of snake that spend their whole lives in the sea. Most are completely helpless on land. They eat fish and other sea creatures, such as shrimp, and all are extremely poisonous. One, the beaked sea snake, has the deadliest poison of any snake.

Which is the biggest snake?

THE WORLD'S LONGEST SNAKE IS THE RETICULATED PYTHON, WHICH LIVES IN parts of Southeast Asia. It grows to an amazing 33 ft (10 meters). The anaconda, which lives in South American rain forests, is heavier than the python but not quite as long. Pythons and anacondas are not poisonous snakes. They kill with their teeth or by crushing prey to death. A python lies in wait for its prey, then creeps up and wraps the victim in the powerful coils of its body until it is suffocated.

Which is the largest lizard?
The komodo dragon, which lives on some Southeast Asian islands. It grows up to 10 ft (3 meters) long and hunts animals such as wild pigs and small deer.

Why does a rattlesnake rattle?
Rattlesnakes make their rattling noise to warn their enemies to stay well away. The rattle is made by a number of hard rings of skin at the end of the tail that make a noise when shaken. Each ring was once the tip of the tail. A new one is added every time the snake grows and sheds its skin.

How many kinds of snake are there?
There are about 2,700 species of snake in the world. They live on all continents except Antarctica, but there are no snakes in Ireland, Iceland, or New Zealand. All snakes are carnivorous—that means that they feed on other animals.

Are all snakes poisonous?
Only about a third of all snakes are poisonous and fewer still have poison strong enough to harm humans. Nonpoisonous snakes either crush their prey to death or simply swallow it whole.

Why do snakes shed their skin?
Snakes shed their skin, or molt, to allow for growth and because their skin gets worn and damaged. In its first year, when it is growing quickly, a young snake may shed its skin seven times or more. After this, it may only molt once a year or less.

Why does a chameleon change color?

CHANGING COLOR HELPS THE CHAMELEON GET NEAR ITS PREY without being seen and allows it to hide from its own enemies. The color change is controlled by the chameleon's nervous system. Nerves cause areas of color in the skin to be spread out or to become concentrated in tiny dots. Chameleons are also said to go darker in color when angry and lighter when afraid.

Chameleon

Are there any poisonous lizards?

There are only two poisonous lizards in the world—the gila monster and the Mexican beaded lizard, both of which live in western North America. The poison is made in glands in the lower jaw. When the lizard seizes a prey and starts to chew, poison flows into the wound. Overpowered by the poison, the victim soon stops struggling.

How many kinds of lizard are there?

There are about 3,000 different species of lizard. These belong to different groups, or families, such as the geckos, iguanas, skinks, and chameleons. There are lizards on all continents, except Antarctica, but most live in warm parts of the world.

Where do chameleons live?

There are about 85 different sorts of chameleon and most of these live in Africa and Madagascar. There are a few Asian species and one kind of chameleon lives in parts of southern Europe.

The python's jaws open extremely wide so it can swallow prey larger than itself.

Do all penguins live in Antarctica?

Most of the 18 species of penguin live in or near Antarctica, but some are found in warmer areas. There are several species around New Zealand, one in the tropical Galapagos Islands and one on South African coasts. There are no penguins in the northern hemisphere.

Which is the smallest penguin?

The little, or fairy, penguin is the smallest penguin – it is only about 16 in (40 cm) long. It lives in waters off the coasts of New Zealand and Tasmania.

Emperor penguins

Which is the biggest penguin?

T HE EMPEROR LIVES IN ANTARCTICA, AND IS THE BIGGEST PENGUIN THE WORLD. It stands about 37 in (95 cm) tall. Like all penguins, the emperor cannot fly, but it is an expert swimmer and diver, using its wings as paddles. It spends most of its life in the water, where it catches fish and squid to eat. Emperor penguins do come to land to breed. The female lays one egg, which the male bird then keeps warm on his feet. The female goes back to the sea, but the male stays and incubates the egg for about 60 days. He cannot leave it, even to feed. The female returns when the egg hatches and cares for the chick while the starving male goes to find food.

What is a tropicbird?

A tropicbird is a seabird with two very long central tail feathers. There are three species, all of which fly over tropical oceans.

The emperor penguin has waterproof feathers and a thick layer of fat to keep out the cold of Antarctica.

Which bird makes the longest migration?

The Arctic tern makes the longest migration journey of any bird. Each year it makes a round trip of more than 25,000 miles (40,000 km). The birds nest in the Arctic in the northern summer and then travel south to spend the southern summer near Antarctica, where food is plentiful.

Why does a pelican have a pouch?

The pelican has a pouch to help it catch fish to eat. When the bird plunges its open beak into the water the pouch fills up with water and fish. As it brings its head up again, the water drains from the pouch, leaving any fish behind to be swallowed.

How many kinds of gull are there?

There are about 45 species of gull. They live in all parts of the world, but there are more species north of the equator. Gulls range in size from the little gull, which is only 11 in (28 cm) long, to the great black-backed gull, a huge 26 in (65 cm) long. Many gulls find food inland as well as at sea and some even scavenge in towns and cities.

How does a gannet catch its food?

The gannet catches fish and squid in spectacular dives into the sea. This graceful seabird flies over the water looking for prey. When it sees something, it plunges from as high as 100 ft (30 meters) above the ocean, dives into the water with its wings swept back and seizes the catch in its daggerlike beak.

Is a puffin a kind of penguin?

No, puffins belong to a different family of birds, called auks. They live in the northern hemisphere, particularly around the Arctic. Auks are good swimmers and divers, like penguins, but they can also fly.

Wandering albatross

The wandering albatross has a strong hooked beak that helps it catch its slippery prey.

Can all seabirds swim?

Not all seabirds can swim. Frigatebirds cannot swim and avoid going into the water. They seize food from the surface or rob other birds of their catches. Storm petrels, too, rarely land on the water, preferring to swoop close to the surface.

Which bird has the longest wings?

THE WANDERING ALBATROSS HAS THE LONGEST WINGS OF ANY LIVING BIRD. When fully spread they measure up to 11 ft (3.3 meters) from tip to tip. This majestic seabird spends much of its life soaring over the ocean far from land and it may travel several hundred miles a day. It lays its eggs and cares for its young on islands near Antarctica.

Can all cormorants fly?

There are about 30 different kinds of cormorant and all but one can fly. The flightless cormorant lives in the Galapagos Islands off the coast of South America. It has tiny wings and cannot fly, but it is an expert swimmer. It catches all of its food in the water.

How fast do penguins swim?

Penguins have been timed swimming at speeds of 6 mph (10 kph), but may move even faster for short periods. They can dive under water for two minutes or more. Emperors are believed to be able to stay under water for more than 18 minutes.

Harpy eagle

The harpy eagle has shorter wings than other eagles so that it can fly among the branches of rain forest trees.

Do eagles build nests?
Yes, and the nest made by the bald eagle is the biggest made by any bird. Some bald eagle nests are up to 18 ft (5.5 meters) deep. They are used again and again and the eagles add more nest material each year.

Which is the fastest flying bird?
As it dives to catch other birds in the air, the peregrine falcon may move at more than 100 mph (160 kph), faster than any other bird. The falcon circles above its victim before making its fast dive and killing the prey with a blow from its powerful talons.

What does an osprey eat?
The osprey feeds mostly on fish. When it sees something near the surface, it dives down towards the water and seizes the fish in its feet. The soles of its feet are covered with small spines to help it hold on to the slippery fish.

Which is the biggest eagle?

THE BIGGEST EAGLE IN THE WORLD IS THE HARPY EAGLE, WHICH LIVES IN RAIN FORESTS in South America. It is up to 43 in (110 cm) long and has huge feet and sharp talons, which it uses to kill its prey. Unlike other eagles, the harpy does not soar high in the air looking for food. It hunts creatures such as monkeys and sloths in the trees, chasing its victims from branch to branch at high speed. Almost as big is the rare Philippine monkey-eating eagle, which lives in rain forests in the Philippines.

Bearded vultures gathering at a carcass

Which is the biggest bird of prey?
The Andean condor is the the biggest bird of prey in the world. It measures up to 43 in (110 cm) long and weighs up to 25 lb (12 kg). Its wingspan is over 10 ft (3 meters).

Do eagles really catch snakes?
Yes, serpent eagles feed mostly on snakes and lizards. The rough surface of the serpent eagle's toes helps it hold on to slippery snakes.

The bearded vulture gets its name from the clump of black bristles that hangs under its beak.

How do eagles kill their prey?
An eagle kills with the four long curved claws on each of its feet. It drops down on to the victim, seizes it in its long talons and crushes it to death. The eagle then tears the flesh apart with its strong hooked beak. The hook of a golden eagle's beak is as much as 4 in (10 cm) long.

How many kinds of owl are there?
There are about 142 different species of owl in two different families. The barn owl family contains about 12 species and the true owl family about 130 species. Owls live in most parts of the world, except a few islands. They usually hunt at night, catching small mammals, birds, frogs, lizards, insects, and even fish.

How can owls hunt at night?

Owls have excellent sight, even in low light, and extremely sharp hearing. Even in complete darkness they can pinpoint where a sound is coming from and swoop. Owls also have special soft-edged wing feathers which make very little noise as they beat their wings. This allows them to approach prey with scarcely a sound.

Do vultures hunt and kill prey?

VULTURES DO NOT USUALLY KILL THEIR PREY. THEY ARE SCAVENGERS, FEEDING on animals that are already dead or have been killed by hunters such as lions. They have strong claws and beaks and the bald head allows them to plunge into carcasses without dirtying their feathers. The bearded vulture, or lammergeier, often picks up bones, which it drops on to rocks to smash them open. It can then feed on the marrow inside.

The bearded vulture soars on its long narrow wings high over remote mountains in parts of southern Europe, Asia, and Africa .

Index